The Little Book of
Body Confidence

52 WAYS TO FEEL GOOD
IN YOUR BODY

JUDI CRADDOCK

First published in 2017 by Judi Craddock.

www.heartyourbody.co.uk

ISBN-13: 978-1975906634
ISBN-10: 1975906632

DEDICATION

In loving memory of my wonderful mother, who always
believed in me.

Contents

Body confidence
doesn't come from
achieving the 'perfect'
body. It comes from
embracing the one
you've got.

Introduction – my story

I first remember feeling uncomfortable in my body at the age of seven or eight years old. I was being teased in the playground for having hairy legs.

I remember the shame, and desperately wanting to be liked and accepted by my peers.

The teasing spread to other aspects of my appearance, like the way I wore my hair and my eyelashes, which the kids said were false.

I tried changing the things that attracted the teasing, using my Mum's razor to shave my legs and getting my long hair cut short. But none of these attempts to change my appearance resulted in greater acceptance by my school mates.

By the age of nine, I believed that acceptance came with conditions. I thought that in order to be liked, I had to look (and behave) a certain way.

This belief has been present for most of my life. It consistently created a self-consciousness about my body and appearance that negatively impacted my life.

I felt that if I could just 'work on' my body to fix all the things that were 'flawed', my life would be happier and more successful.

I allowed body dislike to keep me in unhealthy romantic relationships, hold me back in my career, and stop me doing or wearing things for fear of showing my body.

It took the end of a relationship eleven years' ago for me to finally see what low body confidence had cost me.

For four years I stayed in an emotionally abusive relationship with a partner who constantly criticised my appearance. His criticisms reinforced the beliefs I had about my 'flawed' appearance.

I felt lucky that he stayed with me despite my imperfections, and feared that he would leave me for someone 'better' looking.

Eventually, a voice deep inside of me starting screaming, *"This is wrong, you need to get out of this."* Looking back, I realise it was my intuition trying to protect me.

As I began to question the way my partner treated me, my intuition told me his behaviour wasn't acceptable for someone who supposedly loved me.

I followed my intuition and ended the relationship. After some serious soul-searching, I recognised the role that poor body image and self-esteem played in keeping me stuck in this unhealthy relationship.

I decided right then that I wanted to improve the way I felt about my body and myself. I realised it was time to step into the life I really wanted, and begin living – for real.

I made it my mission to learn everything that I could about confidence and feeling comfortable in my skin. I read books, I had coaching, I trained as a coach and I tried out many, many different tools, strategies and techniques.

Today, I use this knowledge and my personal experience to help my clients and community develop a better relationship with their bodies. A relationship that is grounded in acceptance and respect.

I now view my body very differently. I see it as a vessel that allows me to go about my day to day life and achieve my dreams. I'm grateful for what my body is able to do and I re-affirm this every day.

I let go of the early messages I absorbed in the playground.

I know that my value is not defined by how I look. I found ways to turn my back on the harmful messages about appearance and worth that are prevalent in society.

I discovered that attempts to physically change your body do not create better body confidence. Feeling comfortable in your skin is something that happens within you. It's a shift in mindset, not a diet, a beauty product, or the latest exercise programme.

Growing in body confidence takes time. It's a continual journey, not a final destination. If you commit to the journey and the work involved (and it does take work!), you will acquire knowledge and strategies along the way to help you navigate body dislike and anxiety.

Nobody can promise that you won't ever feel hate or dislike for your body again. But if you are committed to the journey, you'll have the tools you need to handle body anxiety quickly, and with greater ease, when it does arise.

On my body confidence journey, I've found that the biggest transformations have been achieved through simple habits practised consistently. If something seems too hard, time consuming, or not enjoyable, it's difficult to keep it up.

That's what motivated me to create *The Little Book of Body Confidence*. My aim is to provide simple, yet effective tools that will help you along your body confidence journey. Some of the tips are little habits to build into your day to day life. Others are short exercises to shift your beliefs about your body, giving you a different perspective. While other tips are focused on creating the right environment in which body confidence can grow.

The tips and tools are designed to be read in any order. You can dip in and out of them at random, or pick out any that resonate with you. Or, if you are a starter/finisher like me, you can read them cover to cover!

At the end of each tool/tip, I've included some questions to help you reflect on what you've learned from the tool, and any action you'd like to take as a result. You might find it useful to have a journal to hand for recording your answers.

It's my wish that, wherever you are on your body

confidence journey, this book will make it that little bit easier to navigate.

Enjoy the journey!

Judi
xoxo

May I appreciate my body in this moment.

1. Trade expectations of your body for appreciation

This idea comes from Tony Robbins. Robbins says that when you feel dissatisfaction or anxiety in your life, it's because things are not working out in line with your expectations.

When you feel down or dissatisfied with your body, it's likely because you are expecting it to look or behave in a certain way. Often these expectations are unrealistic. For example, perhaps you're comparing your body to a model in a magazine or a younger version of you?

Tony Robbins suggests that when dissatisfaction strikes, you trade the dissatisfaction for something you appreciate.

So when you are feeling unhappy about your body in some way, firstly, stop to notice this dissatisfaction. Ask what expectation is leading you to feel this way?

Then, trade the expectation for appreciation about your body. What can you appreciate about your body right now? Think about what it allows you to do each day. Maybe it's fought off a cold, allowed you to run around after the children, or to do some form of exercise.

The next time expectations of your body leave you feeling down, try this out and notice what a difference it makes.

Using this technique regularly will help you to develop a new found appreciation for the skin you're in.

Reflection Questions:

What expectations do you regularly have about your body?
How does using this technique make you feel about your body?
What have you found to appreciate about your body?

You won't find body confidence in a women's magazine.

2. Do a media detox

A media detox is where you identify any media that is causing you dissatisfaction or anxiety about your body. You then decide to either cut down on, or eliminate that media altogether.

The first step to a media detox is to write down any media that triggers body dissatisfaction. For example, you might find that some imagery in magazines makes you feel unhappy with your body. Or, it could be that some of the people you follow on social media post things that trigger negative body thoughts.

"Growing up, I didn't look at fashion magazines or watch TV. It was healthy - I wasn't comparing myself to anyone."
Christina Hendricks

When I did this exercise, I noticed that the gossip magazines I read were triggering body shame. Reading body shaming content about celebrities made me feel bad about my own body.

Once you've identified any triggering media, cut down on,

or remove it completely from your life for two weeks.

At the end of the two weeks, review how you feel about your body. Have you noticed less anxiety, or dissatisfaction? I bet you will notice some difference! You see, it's very easy to be affected by media that you are constantly exposed to.

Reflection Questions:
What media triggers body dissatisfaction or anxiety for you?
What media are you going to cut down or eliminate?
How has the media detox affected your body confidence?

Food is not 'good' or 'bad'. Food is just food – fuel for the body.

3. Create mantras to deal with holiday body anxiety

Have you ever felt anxious being around food during holidays such as Christmas, Easter or Thanksgiving? Perhaps you've feared putting on weight over the holidays. Or maybe it's the weight or diet talk at the dinner table that creates anxiety for you.

Holidays spent with family and friends celebrating over a large meal can, for many women, be a trigger for body anxiety.

To help you deal with body anxiety during these holidays, it's helpful to have some body confidence mantras at the ready.

If you notice negative body thoughts coming up for you around food or weight talk at the dinner table, try these three steps:

Step 1 - Notice the negative thought and observe it, but don't engage with it. Try saying to yourself, *"Although I'm having this thought, I'm not triggered by it."*

Step 2 - Have a pre-prepared body confidence boosting mantra that you repeat in your head like:

"I'm just really thankful to have food to eat and to be able to spend time with family today."

"No food is 'good' or 'bad', all foods fit into a healthy diet."

"The only reason I should ever feel guilty about eating (insert whatever you feel bad about eating) is if I stole it!"

Say your mantra in your head and repeat it until you feel more positive. You may even want to say your mantra as a statement to others when they engage in diet or weight based talk.

Step 3 - Be proud of yourself for dealing with your body anxiety head on and focus on enjoying the time you have with family and friends.

Reflection Questions:

What's your body confidence boosting mantra for the holidays?

How does using your mantra make you feel about your body?

Losing weight is NOT your life's purpose.

4. Don't diet

Simply do not diet, EVER!

Don't make it one of your New Year's resolutions, don't diet to get a 'bikini body' or to get your pre-pregnancy body 'back'.

There is overwhelming evidence that diets do not work. Ninety-five percent of them fail and most people end up regaining all the weight they lost plus more. Plus, they make you feel miserable and don't improve body confidence, quite the opposite!

> ### "I'm not going to miss ninety-five percent of life to weigh five percent less."
> ### Dan Pearce

The diet industry is predicted to be worth $206 billion by 2019. If diets really worked, the industry wouldn't exist anymore, since we'd all be the 'ideal' weight. Don't be fooled, diets create profits, not body confidence.

Instead of focusing on weight loss as a goal, why not focus on your health? Health isn't about achieving a certain weight or shape. It's more holistic than that. It's about having good mental as well as physical health.

To focus on your health instead of weight, try these steps:

Step 1 - Ask, how do you want to feel in body and mind? Do you want to have more energy, feel calmer, stronger, or more flexible? Write this down.

Step 2 - Write down all the things that you've tried to improve your health in the past year. How did they make you feel? Did you enjoy them? Were they helpful? Make a note of anything that you loved and helped you to feel the things you noted down in Step 1.

Step 3 - Brainstorm a few ideas of how you can achieve the health priorities you wrote in Step 1.

Step 4 - Note down one or two things that you are going to take action on to work on your health. Make sure they are things you will enjoy and that you can make time for.

Go do them!

Reflection Questions:
What's your top priority for your health?
What's one thing you can do right away to move you closer towards that priority?

Scales can't measure the most important things about you.

5. Ditch your bathroom scales

Women have been brainwashed into believing that their weight or dress size determines their value. Weighing yourself each day reinforces this myth.

When I weighed myself each day, the number I saw on the scale had the power to determine how I felt. My mood would vary depending on whether I thought the number on the scale was 'good' or 'bad'.

Don't allow your self-worth to be dictated by a number. You are more than a number on a scale. Scales can't measure your mental health, happiness, personality or achievements.

"The scale can only tell you what you weigh; not who you are."
Steve Maraboli

Plus, if you're thinking that your weight determines your health, think again. Weight in isolation is a flawed way of assessing health. For example, it doesn't take into account what's happening inside your body. It can't, for example, tell you about the health of your lungs, liver, bones, etc.

If you're someone who weighs yourself regularly, try this

three step experiment for at least a week:

Step 1 - Either ditch your scales or put them out of sight.

Step 2 - Don't weigh yourself! Instead notice how your body feels each day. Do you feel full of energy or tired? Listen to your body – what does it need right now? Do you need to rest, go for an invigorating walk or eat something that will give you energy?

Step 3 - After a period of not weighing yourself, notice if you feel any different about your body. Do you feel more at peace and ease?

When I stopped weighing myself I felt better in both mind and body - calmer and more accepting of the skin that I'm in.

Give this experiment a try, and I guarantee you'll notice a difference in how you feel.

Reflection Questions:
How does it feel to ditch the scales?
What difference does ditching the scales make to the way you feel about your body?

Wear clothes you

LOVE

that fit your body

NOW.

6. Get rid of clothes that don't fit

Most women have clothes hanging in their wardrobes that are too small for them. I get it. It's tempting to hold onto smaller items in the hope that one day you might fit into them again.

But when you do this, subconsciously you tell yourself that your body isn't acceptable as it is, with those smaller items of clothing serving as a constant reminder.

If you want to feel more comfortable in your skin, what hangs in your wardrobe should represent who you and your body are **today** (not last year, or before you had a baby).

I only ever keep clothing in my wardrobe that I like, I wear often and fits me NOW. This really helps me to accept the skin I'm in.

If you've got clothing lurking in your wardrobe that you know is too small, try this three step de-clutter process:

Step 1 - Pull everything out of your wardrobe and be honest with yourself about what does and doesn't fit (including things that are too big as well as small).

Step 2 - Remove anything that doesn't fit – give it to charity, re-cycle or sell it. If you really can't face parting with an item, get it out of the wardrobe and pack it away out of sight. Make sure to come back to the item(s) in three to six months' time to see if you are willing to let them go.

Step 3 - Notice any difference in how you feel about your body after the de-clutter. Do you feel more comfortable or accepting of your body each day when you get dressed?

I promise that a wardrobe containing only clothes that fit you (and you like) will make picking out an outfit less stressful and more pleasurable, and you'll experience greater body acceptance.

Have fun with this de-clutter process.

Reflection Questions:

What clothing do you have that you know is too small (or big)?
How does it feel to let go of clothes that don't fit?
What impact did the de-clutter have on your body confidence?

Body hate is something you've learned from the industries that *profit* from body dislike.

7. Stop buying beauty products you feel you *should*

My top beauty tip for better body confidence is to stop buying beauty products you feel you *should* or *must* to look a certain way.

A few years ago, I bought a beauty product called *Baby Skin* that promised pore-free skin. The in-store promotion made me very aware that 1) I didn't have pore free skin and 2) I *should* have!

Looking back now, it seems ridiculous that I believed I should have skin like a new born baby, but that's the power of marketing.

The product's advertising triggered the insecurities I had about my skin. I bought it because I felt I *should* have pore free skin, and because I didn't, I felt inadequate.

Any product that creates feelings of insecurity or inadequacy is not worth buying. In all likelihood, the product won't deliver on its promise (the *Baby Skin* didn't by the way – no surprises there), and you'll feel even worse about your looks.

There are plenty of beauty products on the market, but not

all of them will leave you feeling inferior or inadequate. I'd recommend cutting out the ones that don't make you feel good about yourself.

Go for the products that you enjoy using and aren't using marketing ploys that prey on your insecurities. Look for the brands that focus on the experiential aspects of using the product (the smell, the texture, the impact on your well-being).

"The beauty industry has a responsibility to present positive images and tell positive stories to women." Leslie Blodgett, creator of bareMinerals

Working towards better body confidence means focusing on what makes you feel good in your skin, not what makes you feel bad. Cutting out the beauty products that you feel you MUST buy to be acceptable is a small but effective change to make.

Reflection Questions:

What beauty products are you going to stop buying to boost your body confidence?

How do you feel about your body having cut these products out?

When you look in
the mirror, learn to
see the *person* inside
your body.

8. Do daily mirror work

Mirror work is the number one body image boosting exercise recommended by experts.

It retrains your brain to think about your body in a more positive and healthy way, helping you to drown out negative body thoughts.

It's a technique that I've used myself and with clients to feel more body confident.

While it's hugely beneficial, when you first get started with mirror work, it isn't always easy. But do your best with it.

Here's how to do it:

Step 1 - Look at yourself in a full length mirror. Do this naked if you can, but if that's too much to start with, try fully clothed and then work towards wearing less and less clothing over time.

Step 2 - Tell yourself at least five (stretch to ten if you can) things that you like about yourself and your body. When thinking about your body, include not just physical aspects, but what your body enables you to do, e.g. *"I like that my strong legs enable me to dance and run."* Include what you like about your personality, skills, and achievements, e.g. *"I'm a kind* *and caring person."*

Step 3 - Write these things down each time. Begin building a cumulative list. Look at this list whenever you need a boost. Don't worry if you repeat things – this just helps to reinforce what you like about yourself.

Step 4 - Repeat this exercise daily. Make it part of your routine. If you've been criticising your body for years, it can take time to re-programme this behaviour, so consistent repetition is key.

Don't forget to be compassionate to yourself while you are doing this work. It won't be easy, but it is worth it. Practised consistently, it will become a habit, and the neural pathways in your brain will actually begin to change.

If you'd like a printable to help with your mirror exercise work, I've put one together that you can access for free at: **https://www.heartyourbody.co.uk/little-book-body-confidence-bonuses.**

Reflection Questions:
What does it feel like to do mirror work?
What benefits do you notice?

Beauty is about *diversity*, not conformity.

9. Create your own definition of beauty

When you accept society's limited view of beauty, you set yourself up for a life of body dissatisfaction, since it's an ideal very few can realistically attain.

Making the choice to decide what beauty means for you gives you greater control over your happiness and well-being, and a boost to your body confidence.

When you think about it, society's definition of beauty lacks any depth (it typically doesn't include inner qualities), or diversity (it holds up one body type as superior without recognising a variety of body shapes).

What a boring way to define beauty! It's fine if we all want to be clones, but difference and diversity is what makes our lives rich and interesting.

So make the choice to create your own definition of what makes a person 'beautiful'. Why not even ditch the word altogether and create your own?

"We need to get more flexible about what constitutes beauty. It isn't a particular... body type; it's the woman who lives in the body."
Victoria Moran

Think about all the wonderful people in your life, what qualities do they possess both inner and outer that makes them 'beautiful' to you?

Make your definition as diverse, fun and bold as you like. Just because society has created a one-dimensional view of beauty, doesn't mean you have to live by it.

I think that F. Scott Fitzgerald put it beautifully in his novel, '*The Beautiful and Damned*':

"She was beautiful, not like those girls in magazines. She was beautiful for the way she thought. She was beautiful for that sparkle in her eye when she spoke about something she loved. She was beautiful for her ability to make other people smile even when she was sad. No, she was not beautiful for something as temporary as her looks. She was beautiful, deep down to her soul."

Reflection Questions:

How do you define beauty?

Who do you know who reflects this definition?

What difference does your definition make to the way you feel about your body?

Move your body because it feels good, not to 'mould' it to a particular weight or shape.

10. Move in ways that feel good for *your* body

When I first got into regular exercise, I found it a bit of a chore. I went to the gym because I felt I *should* and because I was worried about gaining weight.

I never really enjoyed the exercise, which made it hard to sustain.

While there is no doubt that regular movement is good for your physical and mental health (which, by the way, includes your body image), if you're forcing yourself to do it, you're not going to keep it up.

"Exercise is a celebration of what your body can do, not a punishment for what you ate."
Women's Health UK

But then I discovered that choosing movement I enjoyed was the key to doing it regularly.

When I started doing activities that I wanted to do, rather than feeling I *should* do them, I stuck to them.

Over the last two years I've taken up a dance class – I love it so much that I WANT to go to it, and it doesn't feel like a chore! At the end of the class I feel amazing – full of energy. And if I'm feeling a little down before the class, I know it's going to lift my mood.

Exercise doesn't have to be gruelling or impossible to be effective for physical and mental health. A brisk walk or even some gardening or housework can do the job. Don't be fooled into thinking you have to embark on some crazy exercise regime to be fit and healthy.

To help you find ways to move that feel good for you, here are three things to consider:

1. **Think back to activities or sports that you enjoyed when you were a kid.** Can you do them now? I danced as a child, so I decided to go back to that. I have a friend who enjoyed netball at school and now plays as an adult.

2. **What activity have you always wanted to take up, but haven't?** Maybe you've always wanted to give yoga or rock climbing a try, but not got around to it? I always wanted to ride a horse, but never learned. Now, at forty-six years old, I'm finally taking lessons!

3. **Are there ways you can move at home or outside at low or no cost?** Movement doesn't have to mean going to the gym or taking lessons. If you like being out in nature, what about a short walk a few times a week? Or maybe you want to try something like Zumba in the comfort of your own home – there are plenty of DVD's, app's and You Tube videos out there.

However you decide to move is fine, as long as it works for you. Don't judge yourself against ridiculous fitness ideals or someone else's activities, do what works for you.

Reflection Questions:
What forms of movement do you love?
What new activities do you want to build into your life?

Ban any word that makes you feel bad about yourself. *'Should'* is one of those words.

11. Stop *'shoulding'* on yourself

(Phrase by Dr. Albert Ellis, Psychologist)

Whenever I catch myself using the word *'should'* it reminds me of something I'm not doing or haven't achieved. In other words, I end up feeling like a failure!

Things like:

"I should see my family more."
"I should be making more money in my business."
"I should make more effort with my appearance."
"I should exercise more."
etc., etc.!

I'm sure you can identify the ways you *'should'* on yourself.

'Should' isn't just a word that impacts your body confidence, it can affect all areas of your life.

"The 'should' shouldn't make you feel bad."
Megan Bearce

'Should' implies that you **must** do something, and somehow

you're not good enough if you don't: lazy, disorganised, out of control.

When you use the word 'should' it's often coming from a voice outside of yourself. You can tell whose voice it is simply by asking, "Who says I should?"

If you say, "I should lose weight." When you ask "Says who?" It's likely coming from family, friends or society telling you that you need to be smaller.

To stop 'shoulding' on yourself, and feeling like a failure or a mess up, try replacing the word 'should' with 'could'.

So, "I should make more effort with my appearance" becomes "I could make more effort with my appearance".

'Could' implies you have a choice, not that you must do something. It allows you to feel more empowered.

It's a simple and subtle change, but it can make all the difference to how you feel. So give this a try.

Think about all the ways you 'should' on yourself when it comes to your body and appearance, and replace that with 'could'.

Reflection Questions:
How often do you use the word 'should'?
How does using 'should' make you feel?
How does it feel turning 'should' to 'could'?
What difference do you notice to your body confidence?

Negative body talk will NEVER give you a *positive* body image.

12. Clean up the way you talk about your body

Do you find yourself saying these kinds of things in conversation?

"I look so old!"
"I'm getting really fat, I need to go on a diet!"
"These flabby arms have got to go!"

If so, it's time you cleaned up your language. If you are saying unkind or unpleasant things about your body around other people, you're not doing your body confidence any favours.

Whatever you verbalise, you internalise, meaning that what you say repeatedly becomes part of your belief system. If you keep saying unkind things about your body, you'll negatively impact your body confidence.

As women we're particularly prone to what body image researchers call 'weight/fat talk' when we get together. It has become a constant topic of conversation, and a way to bond. But as intelligent women with far more to offer than our looks, surely we have more interesting things we could be talking about?

If you want a way to give your body confidence a boost, try these steps to help you stop the weight/fat/ugly talk:

1. The next time you and/or a friend says something derogatory about your/their body, just **become aware that it's happening**.
2. **Notice how the words make you feel.** Do you feel good about your body? It's unlikely you'll be feeling positive about it.
3. **Challenge the words used.** Are they necessary or helpful? (Not really, as they don't make you feel good!). Are they funny? (Is poking fun at women's body parts really that funny?).
4. **Change the conversation**. Make a pact with yourself to focus on topics of conversation other than weight, shape or appearance. If necessary, tell friends you'd rather talk about something else and point out that there are lots more interesting things to talk about. Women aren't just ornaments!

Negative body conversations have been linked to body dissatisfaction in research, so choosing to make this change really can have a positive impact on your body confidence.

Reflection Questions:
What unkind things do you say about your body in conversation?
How does it feel to clean up the way you talk about your body?
What difference do you notice in the way you feel about your body?

Your body *knows*

what it needs

if you will only

***listen* to it.**

13.   Trust your body

Trusting your body means listening to your body's cues, like hunger, fullness, or the need to rest.

When you trust your body, you get to know what feels natural and normal for YOU. Like any relationship, trust is essential for a healthy one, and the relationship you have with your body is no exception.

But it's easy to believe that your body can't be trusted. It can't be trusted to know what, when and how much to eat, or how to move and when to rest.

That's because society is full of voices telling you what your body *should* and *shouldn't* be doing.

Because there is so much noise out there you either can't hear, or don't trust your body to let you know what it needs.

The trouble with those voices is that they have their own agenda – which is usually about getting you to buy something – a diet, an exercise regime, a beauty product or treatment.

It's in their own interest for you to ignore any natural signals from your body and to choose to rely on what these products or services are telling you to do.

What did we do in the days before mass media started telling us what to do? What happened when man lived in caves? Well, we had to trust our instincts.

That's what I'd like you to try. Start trusting your body's instincts and listen to what it's telling you. Here's how:

Step 1 - Make a conscious effort to notice signals from your body e.g. hunger, thirst, tiredness, fullness, feeling unwell.

Step 2 - Ask - what is my body trying to tell me? E.g. I need to eat, drink, take a break, or stop eating.

Step 3 - Be aware of any external voices trying to contradict what your body is saying, e.g. *"You can't eat now, that's not in your diet plan." "I can't stop exercising now, I have to push through this programme."* Don't allow the voices to overrule your trust in your body.

Step 4 - Tell yourself, *"My body knows best."* Even if you don't totally believe that now (remember you've been conditioned not to trust your body).

Step 5 - Honour your body by doing what it's asking e.g. eat, drink, take a nap, whatever it is. Do this as consistently as you can for at least a week.

I know it may feel strange at first. All those voices will come up to tell you that you mustn't trust your body, but persevere until they disappear.

I guarantee if you keep up this practice, you'll notice a difference in how you feel in your body. When you honour what your body needs, you'll experience greater comfort and ease in your skin.

Reflection Questions:
How does it feel to trust your body?
What did you find difficult/easy?

Judgement of others is judgement of *yourself* in disguise.

14.   Stop judging other people's bodies

If you judge other people's bodies, it's actually no different from judging your own. You might think that passing an unfavourable judgement on someone else's body isn't going to do your body confidence any harm. Think again.

That's because it's the same voice inside your head that is harsh towards YOUR body AND other people's. The harsher you judge other people, the harsher it's likely you are towards yourself.

If you can train yourself to be less judgemental of other people's bodies, you'll start to be kinder to your own.

Here are four ways you can suspend judgment of others to be kinder to them and yourself:

1.   **Focus on the person, not the body.** If you know your default is to look at a person's appearance first and foremost, try focusing on what they're like as a person. What is engaging about that person? It might be their friendliness, kindness or warmth.

2.   **See every body as unique.** Avoid the urge to compare bodies against arbitrary 'ideals'. Look at bodies with a different filter – that each and every body is unique.

No two bodies are exactly the same. Each body is okay as it is. It doesn't require assessment. It just is.

3. **Challenge your judgements.** If you catch yourself appraising someone else's body, ask yourself what's really going on? Is this a judgement of yourself in disguise? If you are deriding someone's weight, it's likely based on your own fear of gaining weight. Continuing to judge other people's bodies damages your own body confidence.

4. **Have a mantra at the ready to deal with these moments.** Try something like: *"Bodies come in a diversity of different sizes and shapes, including mine, and that's okay."* Or, *"I'm learning to appreciate body diversity."*

Give these different ways of suspending judgement a try and notice the difference it makes to your body confidence.

Reflection Questions:
How does it feel to stop judging other people's bodies?
Does it make you feel better about your own?

Your body is NOT public property. Nobody has the right to comment on it.

15. Don't tolerate unwanted body comments

One BIG lesson I've learned about body confidence is that even when you accept your body as it is, not everyone will.

Part of being body confident is continuing to value your body even when others don't. This sometimes means you have to call others out on their behaviour.

I'm guessing that you may have been on the receiving end of unwanted comments about your body at some point in your life. I certainly have!

Most unwanted comments tend to focus on weight, for example, when well-meaning family or friends say they are 'concerned' about your health because you are over or under weight (in their opinion).

"Negative comments about your body aren't about your body, they're about society's narrow definition of a 'good' body."
Golda Poretsky

Your body is undeniably your business, and when someone passes unwanted comments, they can be extremely hurtful not to mention unhelpful to your body confidence.

If you're struggling with friends or family who think it's their right to pass comment on your appearance, here's a three step process to deal with it:

First, calmly and confidently tell the person that you find their comments hurtful by being factual but not accusatory, e.g. *"Recently you've often mentioned that you think I ought to lose weight. I want to talk to you about your comments and how I feel about them."*

Then, express how you feel about the behaviour using 'I' statements such as, *"When you make jokes about me being fat, I feel hurt."* Avoid saying how their behaviour 'makes' you feel – this casts blame and will put them on the defensive.

Finally, ask for the change that you'd like to see in their behaviour, for instance, *"I'm asking that you stop talking about my weight."*

If the behaviour doesn't change, ensure there are consequences. For example, you might stop seeing that person until they stop the unwanted comments.

Standing up to comments can mean taking difficult decisions. Sadly, it sometimes means letting a friendship go that has become toxic and no longer serves you.

Reflection Questions:

Who do you need to challenge for their comments about your appearance?

How does it feel to use this process?

How does it feel to stand up for your body?

Your body is where you LIVE. Take care of it, because you only have ONE.

16. Practise self-care

Self-care is taking time out of your day to do things that you enjoy and make you feel good. Self-care doesn't have to take long – even a few minutes each day will do.

Regular self-care helps to build self-worth because it reinforces that you are worthy of care and attention. And when applied to the body, (it can be anything that makes your body feel cared for) is a great way to boost your body confidence.

But, let me be clear – self-care for your body doesn't mean you *have* to look after your *appearance* by hitting the beauty salon and getting yourself plucked, preened and buffed up. Although if going for a beauty treatment is something that makes you feel cared for, that's great.

Your self-care practices can be anything that enhance your well-being in body and mind.

Here are some ideas of ways to up your self-care:

Meditate. It doesn't have to be for long, and it doesn't have to be complicated. Just sitting for five minutes breathing in and out and focusing on your breath is enough each day.

Simple pleasures. Self-care doesn't have to be a grand

gesture. Think of little things you can do during the day to take some time for yourself. I love taking myself out for a coffee and reading the paper, if only for ten minutes. You could go for a quick walk, play with your cat, watch something on Netflix, write your thoughts in a journal or sit reading a book – whatever works for you.

Pampering. What ways can you show your body some love (and it's not about getting your body to look a certain way, it's about what will make it *feel* good)? It could be a hot bath or shower, a good stretch, a massage.

Gentle movement. Walking and practices like yoga and Thai Chi allow you not only to gently move your body, but to quieten your mind, leaving you feeling relaxed and refreshed afterwards.

These are just a few self-care ideas. There are many different ways to practise self-care, and it's up to you to decide what works best for you.

I think self-care is so important to body confidence. Building in little ways to care for your body and mind each day will help you to see not only your body, but your whole self as worthy and valuable.

Reflection Questions:
What are your favourite self-care practices and how can you bring more of them into your life?
How does it feel to take time out to care for your body?

May I be kind to myself in this moment.

17.   Be self-compassionate

Being self-compassionate means being kind and forgiving to yourself.

Compassion is essential on your body confidence journey. In fact, I'd say that a positive body image is more about compassion than confidence.

Along the journey, you'll have times when you feel great about your progress. You'll notice a positive shift in how you feel about your body, then BAM! Something will happen to knock your confidence e.g. you'll receive a hurtful comment about your appearance, compare your body to someone else's or your jeans won't fit. You'll feel right back at square one again with your negative inner voice on overdrive - unless you can be compassionate.

Compassion is the voice that says at those tricky times, *"Hey, you know what? You've come this far. There are going to be challenging times, but that's part of the journey. Everyone goes through this. It doesn't feel nice, but it will pass."*

To help you practise self-compassion, I've got a wonderful process for you to try. It will help you deal with that negative inner voice when it kicks in.

It's a process recommended by Dr Kristin Neff, a well-respected expert on self-compassion.

When you hear that negative inner voice saying you're fat, ugly, old or whatever, here's what to do:

Acknowledge what your inner voice is saying. Neff says that the purpose of the inner voice is to keep you safe. It's therefore important to acknowledge what it's saying, so it doesn't keep shouting louder and louder to be heard. For example, you might say, *"I hear what you are saying, and I know you are only trying to help, but I'm going to try another way to feel better."*

Tell yourself that it's hard to experience such unpleasant thoughts. You might say, for example, *"It's really hard to feel this shame about my body."*

Reassure yourself that you aren't alone in having negative feelings. Realising that you aren't alone in your feelings makes them part of a shared human experience. You might say something like, *"I know I'm not the only one that sometimes feels this way, it's part of life to experience this kind of emotion."*

Finish by asking yourself for kindness. You might say something like, *"May I be kind to myself in this moment."*

Neff also recommends using a physical gesture while going through these steps, such as placing your hand on your heart – this helps to lower the stress levels that accompany negative feelings.

Reflection Questions:

How does it feel to be self-compassionate?
What difference do you notice in the way you feel about your body?

Thoughts are NOT reality. Don't believe *everything* you think.

18. Don't confuse thoughts with reality

When negative thoughts about your body are running riot in your head, it's easy to believe they are true.

On average you have around 60,000 thoughts a day – a staggering ninety-five percent of those thoughts are habitual, with eighty percent of them being negative.

Unfortunately, your brain is hard-wired to pay more attention to negative rather than positive thoughts. This is called **negativity bias**.

But just because you think something, it doesn't make it true. Negative based thinking alerts us to potential dangers, rather than absolute realities.

As Tony Robbins said, *"Our brains are made to keep us safe, not happy."*

This is exactly the role of negative thinking – to keep you safe. While negativity bias helped alert cave men and women to the threat of being eaten by a dangerous animal, it's less useful in modern society.

Today we are less concerned with being eaten and more concerned with belonging.

In a society that teaches women that to be valued you must

look a certain way, it's no wonder that your brain keeps telling you that you need to be thinner or prettier if you want to be loved and accepted.

Just being aware of your brain's tendency to focus on the negative can help you move past these thoughts – to not believe everything that you think.

"Just because I think it, it doesn't make it true."
Mallory Moss

The next time you notice a negative thought about your body, acknowledge the thought is happening and let it pass, remembering that it's your brain's negativity bias at work.

Understanding the brain's bias has helped me to view my thoughts in a different light. When negative thinking arises, I listen to the thoughts, but don't automatically believe them.

Reflection Questions:
How often do you experience negative thoughts about your body?

How do you feel knowing about 'negativity bias'?

What will you do the next time you experience negative body thinking?

You and your body are going to be together for the rest of your life - you may as well be friends.

19. Be your body's best friend

When you think about your best friend, how would you describe your relationship? Best friends are supportive and kind towards each other. Your best friend is usually the person you turn to when you're feeling low.

To create a better relationship with your body, you need to start viewing 'her' as your 'best friend'. When your best friend is feeling down about herself, what do you do? Maybe you offer some words of encouragement, a hug or a listening ear.

But when it comes to your body, perhaps you're not the best of friends. Whenever you say or think something negative about your body, or punish her in some way, you're not being a good friend to her.

Think about it, if you said or did to your best friend some of the things you say, think or do to your body, you wouldn't have a best friend anymore!

"If you talked to your friends the way you talked to your body, you'd have no friends left."
Marcia Hutchinson

To become your own best friend, apply what I call the 'best

friend filter' to everything you say, think and do when it comes to your body.

For example, would you say to a friend that they're ugly or disgusting? Would you force your best friend to do a punishing exercise routine when she was clearly exhausted? I'm guessing not, so what makes it okay to treat your body in this way?

Using the best friend filter will help you be kinder and more supportive towards your body.

If you like, use your *actual* best friend as the filter. Why not buddy up with your bestie to talk about the thoughts you're having about your body to get some much needed perspective?

Reflection Questions:

How does it feel to be your body's best friend?
What difference does it make to your body confidence?

Whatever you can *visualise*, you can *realise*.

20. Visualise your body confident self

Visualisation is a powerful tool that will help your body confidence in two main ways.

Firstly, it allows you to experience what it's like to be your body confident self. This can be incredibly motivating on your journey. It allows you to see what your life will be like with better body confidence.

Secondly, visualisation is a tool that can be used to re-wire your brain. For example, visualisation is used by professional athletes to help boost confidence and results. And research suggests that your brain can't distinguish between something you've actually done, and something that you've visualised, making it an extremely powerful tool.

So if you're someone who has got caught up in negativity about your body, regularly visualising your most body confident self can help create new neural pathways in your brain. These pathways will help you automatically experience more positive feelings about your body.

Here's how to start visualising your body confident self:

Step 1 - Imagine you are your body confident self, and write down:

What am I doing?
What am I thinking?
What am I feeling?

Imagine all the activities you will be doing (that maybe you avoid now) like going swimming, wearing brightly coloured clothing, or enjoying intimacy with the lights on.

Notice what your thoughts focus on. For example, you might be thinking about what you like about your body or what you're grateful for.

Experience how it feels to be your most body confident self, e.g. liberating, carefree, fun, and joyful.

Step 2 - Select a specific activity or scenario from your list.

For example, walking on the beach in your bikini. Close your eyes and experience what it's like to do that activity as your most body confident self.

Notice what your body confident self thinks and feels.

For example, *"It feels great to feel the sun on my skin, I feel at peace and ease in my body."*

Step 3 - Visualise your body confident self each day in the same or different situations.

Do this daily for as long as you want! The longer the better. Notice if the body confident you in your visualisations is becoming the everyday you.

This is a powerful tool that if you keep doing it, will create a more positive attitude to your body.

I love visualisation, and I hope you do too.

Reflection Questions:
How does it feel to be your most body confident self?
What difference do you notice to the everyday you from doing this visualisation?

Forget the fashion 'rules'.
If you like it.
If it makes you feel good.
WEAR IT!

21. Wear whatever the hell you want

That's right, wear what you want! This means you don't care about what the fashion rules say about what you *should* and *shouldn't* wear for your body shape.

In fact, the only criteria you need apply to your clothing choices are 1) do you like the item and 2) do you feel good in it?

If you can say YES to both, wear it!

The most important person to consult when you're making clothing choices is YOU. It's YOUR body and YOUR life, not anyone else's.

Don't get caught up in any 'rules' for dressing. Inflexible rules aren't good for your body confidence, because they teach you that something about your body is unacceptable. These are the kind of rules that say, "Pear shaped (or whatever) can't wear skinny jeans", the sub-text being *"Because your thighs are too big, which doesn't look nice in skinny jeans."*

In my twenties and thirties I wouldn't wear a mini-skirt, because according to the fashion rules, my upper legs were too 'chunky'. But, I liked mini-skirts. I tried them on and liked how they made me feel. But I let fear of my body being judged stop me from wearing them. Fast forward to my forties and I don't have a problem with putting a short skirt on – I've disregarded the rules!

If you're not wearing something you really like because you've convinced yourself your body isn't good enough, you are effectively body shaming yourself.

Take some time to think about any clothing you've stopped yourself from wearing. Maybe you tried something on, loved it, but then talked yourself out of it for fear of being judged for wearing it? If you like the item and feel good in it, what is stopping you from wearing it?

If you're allowing rules or judgement to hold you back, don't. Put that clothing on, get out and carry yourself with pride! And watch your body confidence soar.

Reflection Questions:
What clothing have you stopped yourself wearing?
What items of clothing are you going to wear from now on that you wouldn't before?

Don't let other people's voices take up valuable space in your head.

22. Get other people's voices out of your head

When you're having negative thoughts about your body, whose voice are you really hearing?

It could be your voice, or maybe it's the voice of a critical family member, partner or someone else.

"You can listen to the voices that say there is something wrong with you. Just don't believe them."
Cheri Huber

Your thoughts are largely determined by your beliefs. And beliefs are a product of what you're exposed to regularly.

Few of your beliefs will be original (sorry!). They're beliefs you've picked up from your family, friends, and society. It's not coming from you – you've just come to accept those beliefs without questioning them.

Many of the beliefs that you have about bodies are unhelpful e.g. *"To be happy I need to be thin."* Or *"To be successful I must be more attractive."* None of them are things you've decided for yourself – they've come from someone or somewhere else, and they are bad for body confidence!

To help you question those beliefs and get the unhelpful voices out of your head, here's what to do:

Step 1 - Always ask whose voice is it? Is it something that you've picked up from a family member that you've come to accept as your own view without question? Maybe it's something you've learned from society. Just knowing that voice doesn't come from you gives you a new perspective on it, which makes it easier to get rid of.

Step 2 - Question the motivation behind the voice. Whether the belief has come from family or society, question what is the motivation for it? For example, if one of your body beliefs is that you need to be thin to be attractive, who benefits from you having that belief? The diet industry for one! If the belief came from a family member, it's likely they struggle with their own body confidence and picked up this unhelpful body belief from somewhere else.

Step 3 - Choose if you want to keep this belief or not. Making choices for yourself is empowering. It means that you have questioned a belief and determined if it's helpful or useful to you. It may be that you've got some body beliefs that serve you well, *"Bodies are not ornaments, they help you do so much."* Other beliefs will not be helpful. If they're not helping you feel good about yourself, do you really want to hold onto them? If you choose to set that belief free, write the belief down on a piece of paper and either tear it up or burn it – it's a symbolic way of ditching it for good!

Reflection Questions:
Whose voices are you allowing to take up space in your head? What beliefs are you choosing to let go of?

Bodies come in different shapes and sizes.

There is NO wrong way to have a body.

23. Expose yourself to diverse bodies

The media is inundated with images of a limited body type, a predominantly thin ideal. Research shows that over exposure to these kinds of images has an adverse impact on body image.

When you are constantly exposed to body types that don't represent your body, it's not surprising if you feel invisible and flawed.

But the good news is that, if you expose yourself to images of women's bodies of different ages, races, size, and shapes, you can IMPROVE your body image.

You normalise what you are constantly exposed to, so make sure you expose yourself to diverse bodies!

Bodies come in different shapes and sizes. There is NO wrong way to have a body.

Here are some ideas of how you can do this:

Notice all bodies. When you're out and about, raise your awareness of all body types. Rather than focusing in on the bodies you perceive to be 'ideal', notice all the other body types. Remember, that typically less than five percent of the population has the sort of body type typically seen in media images.

Follow body positive advocates on social media. While much of what you see on social media can be damaging to body image, choosing to follow body positive accounts can have the opposite effect. Body positive advocates accept ALL body types and show images of all bodies.

Take your own photos. If you enjoy taking your own photos or have a creative streak, why not take some photos of your friends and family and create a Pinterest board to show case diverse women's bodies? It's not easy on-line to find images that are diverse, so the more we can all do to put representative images out there, the better it will be for our collective body images.

Reflection Questions:

What are you going to do to expose yourself to diverse body shapes?

How do you feel about your own body having seen a greater diversity of bodies?

The older I get, the less I care about what other people think.

24. Be your ninety year old self

My Grandma is ninety-six years old, and I think she's pretty amazing. Although she's forgetful, she can still move about, and her body is still working.

When I talk to my Grandma, she's amazed that she is still here, but grateful for that. When she thinks back on her past, she doesn't wish she'd been thinner or more beautiful. She does wish that she'd had more time with my Grandpa and two of her children who have already passed away.

Reaching older age is a real privilege, and one that can bring much needed perspective.

So if we could access that wisdom and perspective now, wouldn't that be great?

I think so. Here's how you can get some perspective on your body from your ninety year old self:

Imagine that you are sitting opposite your ninety year old self, and you can ask her whatever you want.

Here are some examples of things you might like to ask her:

What advice would you give me about feeling confident in my body?
How important is being thin/pretty/attractive?

What are your biggest regrets?
What is your most valuable life lesson?

Write down your answers to these questions and anything else you want to add. What did you discover?

When I did this exercise for myself, I discovered that one of the best ways to feel confident in my body now is to be grateful my body works.

I also learned that looks are fleeting, so relying on them is no way to sustain self-esteem or worth.

Finally, my regrets would be about things that I didn't do that I wanted to, like achieving my dream of writing a book (Yah, tick!). I wouldn't be sitting in my rocking chair lamenting the fact that I wasn't thinner or more beautiful.

Try this exercise for yourself, it's really so powerful, and will give you a much needed perspective on your body.

Reflection Questions:

What did you learn from your ninety year old self about body confidence? About life?

How will you think/feel/act differently as a result of what you learned?

Spend your time
with people who
build you up, not
who put you down.

25. Choose who you hang around with carefully

When you're on a journey to better body confidence, it's important to make sure that your environment is supportive.

A big part of your environment is the people that you spend time with. The people you hang out with really do have an impact on how you feel about your body.

It's hard to stay positive about your body when you're surrounded by people who are constantly talking about their weight, critiquing other women's bodies, or worse still, commenting on yours.

"I have insecurities of course, but I don't hang out with anyone who points them out to me."
Adele

It's a harsh reality, but if you have people in your life who are dragging your body image down, it's time to assess how much (or even if) you want to spend time with them.

Here's how:

1. **Think about the people you spend time with**. Does interacting with any of them leave you feeling bad about your body? If so, what are they doing or saying?

2. **What are your options?** How might you deal with someone who is dragging down your body confidence? For example, would this person be supportive if you told them how their actions affect you? Is the person just an acquaintance that you can limit your contact with?

3. **Take action.** Decide what you are going to do. Be mindful that you may not get a positive reaction from someone when you tell them, for example, that you don't want to talk about weight anymore. It may mean that you have to take the difficult decision to stop all contact with them, at least until they can respect your wishes.

If you're finding it difficult to deal with people passing comments about your body, you might also want to read **Chapter 15 - Don't tolerate unwanted body comments.**

Reflection Questions:
Are there people in your life who are bringing your body image down?
If so, what are you going to do?

Striving for the 'ideal' body will never give you the body confidence you seek.

26. Let go of your ideal body

Do you have an ideal of what you'd like your body to look like?

Are you focused on ways that you can achieve that body through diet, fitness programmes or beauty treatments?

Do you believe that once you've achieved your ideal body your life will be happier, more fulfilling or successful?

If you're holding onto the ideal of your perfect body and how amazing life will be once you have it, you aren't really living, because your happiness is **conditional** on having this 'perfect' body.

Pining after and striving for the perfect body means that you don't accept the one that you're in.

"I'm not going to sacrifice my mental health to have the 'perfect' body."
Demi Lovato

Let me be clear – being comfortable in your skin only happens when you can accept your body **as it is. Exactly** as it is. Body confidence isn't about putting conditions on what makes your body acceptable.

To be comfortable in your skin, you need to let go of your ideal body. This means ditching the assumptions you have about your body dictating happiness.

And I've got a simple exercise you can use to ditch your ideal body.

I want you to ask yourself: **How has your ideal body been serving you?**

When you really think about it, chances are, it hasn't served you at all! It's been leading you on a merry dance of time and money wasted counting calories or obsessing about your body.

And while you've been doing all of these things, you haven't been doing other things you'd love to do.

Make a list of all the activities or experiences you've missed out on by chasing your ideal body. For example, not going swimming or wearing your bikini on holiday because you didn't have the 'perfect' body.

List all the emotions you've wasted too like worry, frustration, anxiety, and shame.

Answering this vital question will give you a clear idea of all the things you've been missing out on chasing your ideal body.

Now make a decision to let go of your ideal body and ask, **what can I do with all this time and energy now?** Then, go do it!

Reflection Questions:
How does it feel to let go of your ideal body?
What are you choosing to do with your time and energy now?

You don't have to like

EVERYTHING

about your body

to be

body confident.

27. Accept your feelings about your body

Many women think that in order to be more body confident, they have to love **every** part of their body. This is a misunderstanding that can make the journey to better body confidence feel like another impossible ideal to achieve.

Building better body confidence is as much about acknowledging and accepting what you don't like as what you do. And it's also perfectly natural to feel ambivalent about parts of your body. That doesn't mean you aren't or can't be body confident.

That's why it's important to get clear about how you really feel about your body.

Bottling up your feelings, or denying how you feel is counter-productive. Resisting them creates more dissatisfaction and emotional pain.

If you acknowledge your truth, it gives you the chance to release those feelings, and I've got an exercise to help you do this:

Write down all your body parts from head to toe: your hair, eyes, nose etc., right down to your feet, then describe each of your body parts as *objectively* as possible, and how you feel about them.

Here are a few things that I wrote about myself as examples:

Hair - long and brunette. I really like my hair. It makes me feel feminine.

Thighs - large and rounded. I sometimes feel self-conscious in a swimsuit.

Hands - long and thin. They're okay. I don't have any strong feelings about them.

This exercise may surprise you. It can help you to see your body in a more balanced way. You'll find that even though there are things you don't like, there are some things you do like and a few that you don't have any strong feelings about.

To help you with this exercise, I've created a printable which you'll find with the book bonuses at: **https://www.heartyourbody.co.uk/little-book-body-confidence-bonuses**.

Letting these feelings out moves you one step closer to accepting your body, so give this exercise a go.

Reflection Questions:
How do you feel about your body as a whole?
What surprises, if any, did this exercise throw up?

Your body is a tool for getting stuff done, not the be all and end all of your existence.

28. Focus on your life, not looks

When you're worrying and obsessing about your body, it can take over not just your thoughts, but your life.

To break that cycle, having a focus away from your body and looks is essential. Research has shown this is a useful body image boosting strategy.

When I decided that I wanted to have a better relationship with my body, I took a good hard look at my life. I realised that there were things that I wasn't happy with. There were things I wanted to do that I had been holding myself back from.

I decided to throw myself into work and projects that would give my life meaning and purpose. I applied for a new role at the company I was working for and signed up for a voluntary project overseas (a lion breeding project in Zimbabwe, Africa).

Focusing on what I wanted to experience in my life not only gave me a great sense of fulfilment, it distracted me from the negative thoughts I was having about myself and my looks.

Doing work that I loved built up my confidence and self-worth. Body worries became less of a concern as I filled my life in other ways. It dawned on me that there was a lot more to life than looks!

I now know that much of my body hate was dissatisfaction with my life wrongly directed at my body. It was easier to blame my body for not having the life I wanted.

To help you get focused on your life, here are some key questions to ask yourself:

Where are you holding yourself back in life? Perhaps your pre-occupation with appearance is keeping you from applying for a promotion, starting your own business or getting back into dating.

What things do you really want to do? Is there something you've wanted to do for a long time but you keep putting off because you don't think you or your body are worthy enough? It could be a hobby, a career change, starting a family, getting married, travelling, whatever.

What will really fulfil you? What will give your life a new focus and purpose that will excite, motivate and inspire you?

What action can you take right now to focus on your life, not your looks? It doesn't have to be anything big. Doing some research on a hobby, trip or job you're interested in is a step forward that can build momentum.

Working towards a life that feels fulfilling and meaningful builds self-worth and self-esteem, which in turn improves body image.

Reflection Questions:
What are you going to focus on in your life?
What's the first step you're going to take to get started?

"Everything will be okay in the end, and if it's not okay, it's not the end."

Anonymous

29. Say, "I'm okay"

Sometimes when negative thoughts are dragging you down, you need something quick and do-able to distract from those thoughts.

The practice of simply saying to yourself *"I'm okay"*, even when you don't believe it is a powerful way to interrupt negative thinking.

Saying *"I'm okay"* gives your brain a new instruction – to look for and experience 'okay' thoughts and feelings.

Repeat this phrase when you wake up, before you go to sleep, when you're experiencing negative thoughts or dealing with a difficult situation.

It will help calm your mind and get it focused on being okay.

That's all you need to do. It may sound simple, but give it a try.

Remember it's the simple, easy to action things that you will consistently keep doing.

Reflection Questions:
How does it feel to say *"I'm okay"*?
What difference does this phrase make to negative thinking?

If you don't

LOVE it

or

USE it,

it's CLUTTER!

30. Get rid of body clutter

Body clutter means any items that you have collected for a body related purpose, like a fitness DVD, exercise bike, or beauty products that you no longer use.

Holding onto body clutter that you don't use can create feelings of guilt. For example, you might start *'shoulding'* on yourself, thinking that you *'should'* be doing that fitness programme or riding your exercise bike. Or you *'should'* be using that anti-ageing cream to stop those wrinkles.

'Shoulds' leave you feeling like a failure, and when it comes to body stuff that you think you *'should'* use, you end up thinking your body is a failure – which is NOT good for your body confidence.

If you haven't already, you might also want to read **Chapter 11 - Stop *'shoulding'* on yourself**.

To prevent body clutter dragging down your body confidence, here's what to do:

1. **Identify any body related items that you haven't used in the last six months**. Ask yourself, realistically, will you use it/them again? Remember that if you never enjoyed using an item, it needs to go! If

riding that exercise bike is something you hate, you aren't going to use it. Find some other way to move your body that you actually enjoy (you might want to read **Chapter 10 – Move in ways that feel good for *your* body,** to help you).

2. **Give the items to friends who might like them, a charity, or sell them.**

3. **Ditch what you don't love.** If a body related item isn't something you love or enjoy using, get rid of it!

Reflection Questions:

What body clutter have you got lurking in your home?
How does it make you feel?
What are you going to do with it?
How does it feel to get rid of body clutter?

Your body is
precious.
Take care of it in
every way
you can.

31. Address body neglect

An important part of building your body confidence is listening to your body, and taking care of anything that needs attention.

When you respond to your body's needs, and take loving care of it, you're showing love and respect for it.

Ignoring what your body needs and not addressing illness or pain is neglect (**Note -** if you find it difficult to tune into what your body needs, you might find reading **Chapter 13 – Trust your body** useful).

If you've been struggling with a niggling back pain, a sore tooth, or maybe you know your eyes need testing, now is the time to seek some help.

Deciding to get help sends a message to your body that it is worthy of care and attention.

Ask yourself, what parts of my body need attention? Where have I not kept up with regular check-ups and appointments? Book them in now.

As women, there are certain checks that we must regularly do like breast screens and cervical smears. I want to urge you to make sure you aren't missing these. With both breast and cervical cancers, early detection greatly increases survival rates.

Show your body it's worth looking after and seek out the care it needs.

Reflection Questions:
What parts of your body have you neglected?
What are you going to do about it?

A *'beach'* body is

YOUR body,

in a swimsuit,

ON

a BEACH.

32. Get your *mindset* beach ready

In the run up to the summer holiday season, we're bombarded with magazine articles and adverts telling us how to get that 'beach body'.

This drives me crazy, and I can be heard groaning, swearing and muttering at these articles and adverts!

It's these kinds of messages that can turn holiday excitement into vacation body anxiety IF you let them.

Bear in mind that the products being advertised as the magic pill for a beach body are feeding off your insecurities, playing on any negative thoughts you might already be having about your body.

Going into the summer season, focus **not** on making your body beach ready, but your *mindset*.

Here are some ways to get your mindset beach ready:

Ditch any media that is promoting the beach body ideal. In the run up to your summer vacation, make sure you aren't exposing yourself to any media prone to beach body make-over madness, whether that's magazines or social media.

Lean into the fear of being seen in your swimmers. Even if you feel afraid of wearing your swimsuit, put it on and head to the beach anyway. It's the fear of what might happen that is greater than the reality. Ask what is the worst thing that can happen? It's unlikely you'll get laughed off the beach, which is the type of irrational fear you can have. Once you can acknowledge the fear, but carry on anyway, you take away its power over you.

Acknowledge that others are busy judging their own bodies. If you fear your body being judged, know that for most people, looking at your body is the least of their concerns – they're too busy worrying about their own.

Focus on the experience. If you get your body out on the beach, what can you experience and enjoy? For example, you might go swimming, feel the sun on your skin, the sand between your toes. Let this be your motivation for getting your swimmers on. Imagine what you would be missing out on hiding underneath a towel or an oversized beach cover up.

Have fun on your vacation. All you need to do to be beach ready is get your swimmers on and GO!

Reflection Questions:
What are you going to do to get your mindset beach ready?

The most important relationship you'll ever have is the one you have with YOURSELF.

33.   Learn to like YOU

With so much focus on bodies and appearance, you can lose sight of the fact that there is a person living inside your body. A person with a personality, skills, and much more.

For many people, body dissatisfaction is dislike of the self, turned on the body.

To appreciate that you are more than a body or an object to be looked at, it's time to start getting to know and like the person inside of you, and I've got one simple but effective way that you can do this.

Create a proud log. Yes, that's right, a 'proud' log. Does that make you cringe? If it does, it's likely that you aren't used to celebrating what makes you special or unique.

Write down **fifty** things that you are really proud of yourself for. Keep going until you get to fifty. They don't have to be grand achievements, but things that are important to you. Every time you think you've run out of things, keep asking, "What else?"

I did this at the start of the year looking back at 2016, here are a few things I wrote:

1.   Helping my Dad clear out his house (my Mum died a

few years ago, and it's taken time for both him and I to come to terms with the loss and be able to clear out her personal possessions).

2. Starting to create videos for my business (there was huge resistance to starting this!).
3. Learning to ride a horse.
4. Getting through a particularly stressful house sale.

Looking back at your proud log gives you an indication of the character traits and skills that make you who you are. So in my case, helping my Dad showed that I had empathy and strength, creating the videos demonstrated courage, and getting through a stressful time showed resilience.

It's not until you take the time to look back on what makes you proud that you realise what you've been able to do, and what it took to do it.

Give this exercise a try, and look back at everything you've written with pride, knowing that this is the real YOU. This is what's important, not your appearance.

Because learning to like yourself is vital to your confidence and self-worth, I've created an additional exercise called, *I am a unique and valuable person*, which you can access with the book bonuses at: **https://www.heartyourbody.co.uk/little-book-body-confidence-bonuses.**

Reflection Questions:

What character traits do you most admire in yourself?
What do you most like about being you?
What are you most proud of?

Happiness comes from helping others.

34. Give to others

Research has shown that when you give to others it releases endorphins in the brain and boosts happiness for you as well as the people you help.

Giving to others is not only good for your happiness, it can also improve your body image. When you focus your attention on others, rather than on your body concerns, it can help protect against body dissatisfaction.

Doing things for others helps distract you from negative body thoughts and concerns, as well as giving you a different perspective on what's important in life.

So why not think about how you can give to others?

Giving doesn't have to be anything huge. It can be a simple act of kindness such as: giving up your seat on a train, letting someone take your parking space or handing on an unused ticket, or planning to spend time with a friend who needs support.

Or if you'd really like to help a cause, why not research ways in which you can help a charity?

I have a friend who is a befriender to an elderly person, calling her on a regular basis to help combat loneliness.

I do education talks for the UK pet charity Blue Cross, to

help young people become responsible pet owners.

There are so many ways that you can give, so find what works for you.

Reflection Questions:

How might you give to others?
How does giving make you feel?

Your life is happening NOW.
Don't put it on hold until you've achieved the 'perfect' body.

35. Stop the 'when...thens'

Let me explain what I mean by the *'when... thens'*. *When thening'* goes something like this:

When I lose 10 pounds, **then** *I'll start dating.*
When I'm a size 10, **then** *I'll start wearing a bikini.*
When I'm in better shape, **then** *I'll apply for the job.*

'When then' is really code for − *"I'm putting my life on hold until I am more acceptable."*

The problem with this approach is that you are making your life, and your happiness conditional on something else.

When it comes to bodies, this is very common. We allow the size or weight of our bodies to dictate what we can and can't do with our lives.

Not only is this very bad for body confidence because you are saying, *"My body is not acceptable right now"*, you are also wasting your life waiting.

To stop the *'when thens'* in their tracks, here's what you can do...

The next time you notice yourself saying *'when then'* in relation to your body, ask yourself:

Can I do that now, just as I am? Is there anything stopping you other than your beliefs about your body?

If I can do it now, why am I procrastinating? What's the fear that's really holding you back? Judgement? Rejection? Own the fear – write it down, say it out loud.

Are my justifications valid, or just an excuse? Sometimes it can be easier to blame your body for not doing things, rather than facing your real fears. For example, using your body as an excuse not to look for a partner because you fear being hurt.

Facing up to the real reason you're holding yourself back takes the power away from the fear and allows you to face it head on. Ask yourself what is the worst that can happen if you started wearing that bikini, joined a dating site or applied for a new job?

Reflection Questions:
What *'when thens'* are present in your life?
What *'when thens'* are you committing to stopping dead in their tracks?

Treat your body like it's someone you LOVE.

36. Treat your body like a lover

Your lover is someone you really care about and want the best for.

When you're in love, you want your partner to feel loved and cherished.

If you hear your partner saying negative things about themselves, you listen to and reassure them.

Having a healthy relationship with your body is much like being in a loving relationship with a partner.

To help you create a more loving relationship with your body, think about your experience of being in a loving relationship, either current or past.

If you find that you are putting yourself down, stop and imagine what you would say to someone you loved doing this.

So if your partner said, *"I'm so fat/ugly/skinny/stupid."* Or *"I hate the way I look"*, how would you respond?

You'd probably try to reassure them and tell them all the things you love about them. You might listen to them and ask what was going on that was making them feel this way.

You'd tell them you love them for who they are. You

wouldn't say, *"Yes, you're right!"*

The next time you catch yourself saying unkind things to yourself, stop for a moment and imagine what you'd say to your partner or lover. Even if you don't believe it, still say it.

This kind of reaffirming self-talk is a powerful and effective tool in developing body confidence.

Reflection Questions:

How would you treat your body if it was someone you really loved?

How does it feel to treat your body like a lover?

Relationships are the single most important factor for happiness.

37. Connect with others

Feeling uncomfortable in your skin can lead you to withdraw from others – particularly if social situations make you feel body conscious.

However, according to the group, **Action for Happiness**, relationships are the single most important factor for happiness. People with strong relationships are happier, healthier and live longer.

For body image, there is evidence to suggest that social support, particularly within a family environment can help protect against body dissatisfaction.

Seeking out the right kind of connection with friends and family can help you feel more comfortable in your skin.

That being said, you do have to select the people that you spend time with very carefully. You want to surround yourself with friends and family who are supportive of your efforts to improve your body confidence – people that you can openly share how you're feeling without judgement, and who don't trigger body anxiety in you.

If you have people in your life who are triggering body anxiety, and you need some help dealing with them, you might want to read **Chapter 15 - Don't tolerate unwanted body**

comments and **Chapter 25 - Choose who you hang around with carefully**.

To make meaningful connections that support better body image, think about who you'd like alongside you on your body confidence journey:

Who do you feel most comfortable with?
Who do you feel most supported by?
Who do you feel will best understand your struggles or concerns?
Who can you talk openly to?
Who do you have fun with and/or share common interests?

Remember that connection is not just about being able to discuss the way you feel about your body, but being able to have some fun times too.

Reflection Questions:
Who can you connect with that will help to boost your happiness and body confidence levels?

If you believe that you *'could'* like your body, then you CAN.

38.   Be open to liking your body

I know that when you're gripped with body dislike, saying things like, *"I hate my body, I don't like anything about it"*, it's a tricky place to be.

You feel stuck, and it's a downward spiral.

If you find yourself stuck in this negative spiral, it's helpful to open up your way of thinking and see new possibilities.

Saying that you *could* like your body, opens you up to the possibility.   Sometimes that is all you need to start thinking, feeling and acting differently.

'Could' is about choice: I can choose to like my body or not. For me, *'could'* always seems to have a certain power to it.   It feels like I am in control.

If I *could* like my body, and I have that choice, why wouldn't I?

If you find yourself saying and thinking that you don't like your body, take a moment to say, *"But I could"*, then notice how you feel.

Do you feel more hopeful?   More in control?

Or maybe you feel that's ridiculous at first… that's okay.   If it's too big a stretch at first, keep saying, *"I could like my body"* each time you think that you don't, and see how different you feel over time.

The language you use is so powerful. Language can totally alter your perspective, so don't underestimate the power of this one small change.

Reflection Questions:

How does it feel to say, *"I could like my body"*?
What difference do you notice in the way you feel about your body?

Growing old is part of
life.
Grow into your
wisdom, and let your
wrinkles tell the story
of your life.

39.   Revere ageing

In Western cultures, we've come to fear ageing, seeing it as something to fight against.

It's like we're at war with our bodies, fighting with anti-ageing this and that.

Our youth obsessed culture associates ageing with a loss of looks, not with any beneficial changes, such as increased wisdom and contentment.

"Ageing is not lost youth, but a new stage of opportunity and strength."
Betty Friedan

But Life is NOT a beauty contest.

You're not better if you 'age well' or 'don't look your age'.

Ageing is something for you to be grateful for, because the only way you stop ageing is by dying!

Age is not a 'battle' to be 'fought'. Growing old is part of life. Grow into your wisdom and let your wrinkles tell the story of your life.

With age, comes greater wisdom and confidence.

I feel more at ease with myself NOW than I have ever done in all my forty-six years. I may not look the same as I did in my youth, but I value the person that I've grown into and all that I have experienced and learned.

In Eastern cultures, age is revered not feared. Older women are valued for their wisdom.

So to help you revere, not fear ageing, I've got one question you can ask yourself that will get you focused on the benefits of age:

What are your most valuable life lessons? These are things that can only be learned with age and experience, but once you get them, they make life easier and happier.

For example, I didn't realise that I couldn't be in a loving relationship with a partner until I loved and accepted myself. It took me to the age of thirty-five to finally get this. And once I did, I finally found love with a wonderful man.

Of course, it would have been useful to know that much earlier, but that's not how life works. You have to learn the lessons for yourself.

I'm so glad that I have this (and other) wisdom now. This is what revering your age is about, tapping into the life experience that makes life that bit better – more peaceful, enjoyable, fulfilling.

Seeing ageing as something far more than the loss of your looks is vital for a happier life and better body confidence.

Reflection Questions:
What do you revere about ageing?
What's one thing you are truly grateful for that age has given you?

The present moment is all you have, so be here NOW.

40.   Be in the moment

Being in the moment means that you aren't mulling over the past or contemplating the future. You may have heard the term mindfulness, which is the practice of 'being in the moment.'

You're fully committed to experiencing what is happening right here, right now.

If you think about it, the present moment is all you really have, since you can't change the past, and the future hasn't yet happened.

Initial research by the **Centre for Appearance Research** looking at the impact of mindfulness on body image found that it can help reduce body concerns.

By paying attention to whatever you are doing in the moment, it takes the spot light off your body.

Mindfulness can reduce both the number of negative body thoughts experienced and the intensity of any unpleasant feelings that come with the thoughts.

Here's a few simple steps to help you bring mindfulness into your day to day life:

Whatever you're doing, bring your full attention to it. It doesn't matter if you're washing dishes, eating or hanging out with friends. Bring all your senses into play – what can you feel, hear, smell, or taste? Really notice everything about the moment.

Let thoughts or judgements of the future or past float away. This is easier said than done, but allow thoughts or judgements to pass by – don't get involved with them. Go back to whatever you are doing and continue to experience it fully.

Be kind to yourself. If thoughts keep cropping up while you're being mindful, don't beat yourself up about it. Being in the moment takes practice.

Reflection Questions:
What does it feel like to practise being in the moment?
What impact does being in the moment have on your body confidence?

Don't worry about what other people are doing. Stay focused on your own journey.

41. Keep your eyes on YOUR journey

Working on your body image is NOT easy work. It takes time, patience, and most of all self-compassion.

When you're on a journey to a better relationship with your body, there are going to be up's and down's. You'll make strides forwards and sometimes backwards.

But that's okay. It's all part of the process.

However, what isn't a healthy or helpful part of the process is comparing your body confidence journey to someone else's.

Doing this is counterproductive, because your journey is as unique as you are.

When we compare, we have a tendency to make upward comparisons – comparing ourselves to someone who appears to be further along their journey than we are. We might ask, *"What's wrong with me, why can't I be like her?"*

I don't want this type of comparison to bring you down along your journey.

So my advice is, **keep your eyes on your own journey.** This means being single minded and focused on what you are doing and not worrying about anyone else.

You will never really know what progress someone else is making anyway. People only share what they want to share, and as we know only too well from social media, this isn't always the full picture.

Compare your **yesterday to today** not someone else's. Look back at how far you have come from when you first started out – be proud of every single success, no matter how small.

Reflection Questions:

How does it feel to compare your yesterday to today?

How does it help your body confidence?

Fat or thin, the size of your body doesn't dictate your worth.

42. Let go of fat phobia

Recently, I surveyed my community about their body confidence. The word 'fat' was repeatedly used by women to describe their bodies.

For most of these women, 'fat' wasn't used as a neutral way to describe their bodies, but an insult.

Fat phobia and fat discrimination are rife in our culture, with women (and men) going to extreme lengths to avoid being fat.

But the simple fact is that fat is just fat. We all have fat on our bodies, some people more, others less. Being fat doesn't make you less worthy, nor does being thin make you more so.

It's the judgements placed on fat that result in body shame.

If you look up the dictionary definition of fat it certainly doesn't say fat is unlovable, ugly, gross or revolting – words that are often associated with fat.

"Fat is not an insult. It is a descriptor. And when you interpret it as an insult, you reveal yourself and what you fear most."
Roxanne Gay

Fat is not a moral indication of who you are or what you can do.

Sadly, there are people who will say unpleasant things about fat and pass judgement, and you can't control what they say.

But you can control your reaction to their words and judgements.

Here are four tips to help you do that:

Remember, fat is just fat. We all have it. Without it, our bodies wouldn't function properly. Fat is a neutral descriptor in the same way that the words 'short' or 'tall' are used to describe someone's height.

Reaffirm to yourself that your worth as a person is not determined by how much or little body fat you have. It doesn't dictate what you can or can't do or be.

Be aware that judgements about fat say more about the person passing the judgement. Unpleasant comments come from a place of ignorance, and very likely personal insecurity about the person's own body.

People who take offence at fat don't have to look! If you are ever troubled by fat discrimination, tell the person it's their problem and they don't need to look!

"It's not my responsibility to be beautiful. I'm not alive for that purpose. My existence is not about how desirable you find me."
Warsan Shire

Reflection Questions:
How do these insights make you feel about fat?
What are you going to do to let go of fat phobia?

Someone else's opinion of you is not your reality unless you allow it to be.

43.   Let go of other people's opinions

There's no doubt that the opinions, comments and judgements of others can have an impact on your self-esteem and body confidence IF you allow them to.

One of the key factors determining the formation of self-esteem and body image is the influence that family (and other authority figures), friends and peers have.

I remember as a child of seven or eight years old being told by a teacher that I'd never amount to much. This stayed with me for years, leaving me with the constant feeling that I wasn't smart or intelligent enough.

So I tried really hard at school to make something of myself to prove the teacher wrong. But this constant striving created perfectionistic tendencies that spread into all areas of my life, leaving me stressed, anxious and lacking in confidence for many years.

During my coach training, while doing an exercise to uncover where my negative self-beliefs had come from, I realised the impact of the teacher's remarks and how unhelpful they'd been (not to mention irresponsible).

I realised I didn't have to take the teacher's comments on board any more. I could let them go.   This was hugely liberating.

To help you let go of other people's opinions or judgements about you or your body, try these three steps:

Step 1 - Write out any comments, beliefs or judgements that have been made by family, friends, colleagues, etc. What beliefs or judgements have left you feeling inadequate about yourself or your body? For example, a family member may have passed judgement about your body or ability (like my teacher did).

Step 2 - Decide if the comment or judgement is helpful, constructive or valid. It's more than likely that it isn't. For example, in my case, it wasn't helpful for my teacher to make that comment about me. Without encouragement, how was I to do well at school? If the comment doesn't help in any way, don't take it on board.

Step 3 - Write out your response to the judgement, opinion or comment. In response to my teacher saying I wouldn't amount to much, I wrote, *"I'm a unique person with my own talents. My life is what I choose to make it."* Keep these responses where you can easily find them. Read over them whenever you feel yourself being triggered by any old, unhelpful beliefs or judgements.

Reflection Questions:

Whose opinions or judgements are you choosing to let go of? What response do you want to make to them?

Saying *one* thing and doing *another* will not give you the outcome you want.

44. Walk your talk

Walking your talk means that your words and actions match.

For body acceptance and respect to take root, what you *say* about your body and the way you *treat* it must be congruent

If you say that you respect your body, you'll make sure that, amongst other things, you take time to rest, feed yourself nourishing foods, and move your body in ways that feel good.

If instead of doing these kinds of things, you put yourself on another punishing diet or exercise regime, you're sending a strong message to your body that you don't respect it. There is a mismatch between your words and actions.

Along the journey to better body confidence, there will be temptations to go back to old habits. You'll start to wonder if maybe losing weight on another diet might just make you feel better about your body.

To help walk your talk, and keep your body confidence growing, I've got one simple question you can ask yourself.

Examine your actions in light of how they impact your body by asking, **does this action show my body I love it?**

For example, it you are exercising to the point where you are in a great deal of pain, does that show your body you care for it?

If you constantly drink to excess, does that show your body that you love and respect it?

If you refuse to rest to the point of becoming unwell, does that show your body you love it?

If you restrict your food intake to the point of exhaustion and overwhelming hunger, does that show your body you love it?

You get the picture. This one simple question is a great filter through which to check your actions against what you say about your body.

For body confidence to grow, your new ways of thinking and speaking about your body need to be backed up by action.

Reflection Questions:
Do your words match your actions when it comes to your body?

If not, what action are you going to take?

Each time you show your body acceptance, respect, or kindness, you help another woman to do the same.

45. Be a role model for positive body image

If you feel like you have a long way to go to be more comfortable in your skin, you may think this tip isn't relevant to you.

But it is!

We live in a society that associates thinness with the 'perfect body' and are constantly exposed to messages that perpetuate this ideal.

However, when you think about it, WE are that society. That means that we can take responsibility for behaving and speaking in ways that promote positive body image.

Speaking and acting in ways that advocate for better body image has a positive impact not only on the body confidence of others, but your own.

Being a role model for positive body image is a win, win situation.

"You don't improve your body image only for yourself. You do it for every other woman out there who is struggling." Summer Innanen

If you're not sure how you can be a role model, I've got a few ideas to get you started:

Think carefully about commenting on someone else's size (either positively or negatively). Negative comments are distressing and not in line with being a positive role model. Although you might think praising weight loss is a positive thing, it perpetuates the thin ideal that acts as a trigger for a lot of negative body image.

Stop criticising your own body or appearance in front of others. Public self-criticism shows others that you don't approve of your own body and encourages others to do the same, worsening body image all round.

Don't join in with body bitching. When you hear a woman talking about how unhappy she is with her body, rather than join in, tell her that she is much more than her size or weight, and ask her to recognise the woman she is on the inside.

Stop body shamers in their tracks. Don't tolerate people who openly body shame others. Call them out on it. Emphasise that other people's bodies are not public property to be judged and commented upon.

When you role model healthy body behaviours, you not only help others, but you boost your own body confidence too.

Reflection Questions:
How will you be a role model for positive body image?
How does being a positive role model impact your body confidence?

What you believe about your body determines how you feel about it.

46. Create empowering body beliefs

Most of the beliefs you have about your body come from others — things you have been told or absorbed from family, friends, and society.

Creating empowering body beliefs is one way to replace the old, unhelpful ones.

If you need help to challenge and let go of old beliefs, then you'll find it helpful to read **Chapter 22 - Get other people's voices out of your head** and **Chapter 43 - Let go of the opinions of others.**

If you want to think about your body in a positive way, you need to create some empowering beliefs about it.

As Tony Robbins says in his book '*Unlimited Power*': "*The trick is to choose the beliefs that are conducive to success and to discard the ones that hold you back.*"

The words that you use to describe your body influence how you think and feel about it, and the way you treat it.

The following exercise is designed to allow you to create empowering body beliefs. Here's how it works:

Firstly, choose three words to describe your body in a positive, kind and uplifting way. For example, when I did this exercise, I chose to use the words: active, strong, and flexible.

Other words you might consider: vibrant, unique, capable, free, comfortable, gentle, happy, relaxed, stylish, calm, sexy, active, amazing, powerful, etc.

Use any words that feel right for you, but remember this is not about using unhelpful, negative adjectives! Even if you don't believe these words to be true for your body now, it doesn't matter. You are *choosing* what you want to believe about your body from now on, which in turns generates new thoughts, feelings and behaviours.

Secondly, write down, *"From this moment, I choose to see myself as ...."* (Completed with the three words that you picked).

Thirdly, repeat it often.

Doing this exercise helps to re-programme your mind for better body image. When you change the beliefs you have, then your thoughts, feelings and actions follow.

Reflection Questions:

What new empowering beliefs have you created about your body?

How do these new beliefs impact the way you feel about your body?

No matter what
your mood, music has
the magical ability
to lift it,
even on a bad day.

47. Choose a body confidence theme tune

Yes, you read that right, a body confidence theme tune!

When you feel down on your body, and your head is filled with negative thoughts, it can be difficult to shift them.

But what if you had a quick way to stop your negative thinking? To give you a moment to reflect on what you're doing and choose a different, more empowering approach?

That's where your body confidence theme tune comes in.

Music can be so powerful. Think about some of your favourite tunes and the emotions they evoke? Or how they transport you to different times, both happy and sad?

Having a tune that you play in your head (or to play or sing out loud if you prefer) when negative thinking starts, interrupts the flow of those thoughts and can be an instant mood elevator.

If you could choose a song to hear when negative thinking kicks in, what would it be? What would make you pause and reflect, or make you feel more empowered or inspired?

When I feel I need a confidence boost, I like to play Katie Perry's 'Roar' in my head.

It reminds me that I have a voice and get to choose for myself what I want, and that I can be strong and powerful. I especially like the line where Perry sings, *"Cause I am the champion, and you're gonna hear me roar."* For me, the roar is about taking control, and being powerful.

This really simple tip is so effective. Select songs to break your negative unhelpful thinking and make sure they are positive and inspiring to you.

Reflection Questions:
What song will most inspire and uplift you when your body confidence is low?
How does it feel to play this song?
What difference do you notice to your body confidence after playing the song?

I believe my body

IS

GOOD.

48. Believe your body IS good

One of the misconceptions about having a positive body image is that you believe your body *looks* good. But this isn't the case.

One person with a positive body image might think their body looks good, another might not. But both can still have a positive body image.

Central to having a positive body image is believing that your body IS good. Viewing your body as a vehicle that allows you to live your life and achieve your dreams.

It's about believing that your body is worth more than looks. It's understanding that your looks don't need to hold you back from doing what you want or being who you want to be.

Your body is what allows you to exist, it's your home, working hard for you each day. Without your body, where would you be?

Your body IS a good thing. There is no right or wrong way to have one.

This is likely a fundamental shift in the way you view your body. I appreciate it can be a tough one to get to grips with after years of being convinced that your body needs to *look* good to be good.

But let this belief sit with you. Write it out. Look at it each day.

I believe my body is good.

How can something that does so much to keep you alive NOT be a good thing?

Think of all the good your body does:

- Fights infection
- Produces children
- Keeps your heart beating 24/7
- Removes toxins
- Heals wounds
- Alerts you to dangers

The list goes on. Why not make a list of all the amazing things that your body does?

Over the next week, every day, repeat the belief, **I believe my body is good**. Notice how it feels.

Reflection Questions:

How does this new belief influence the way you feel about your body?

Set yourself free from difficult emotions about your body by forgiving *yourself* and *others*.

49. Practise forgiveness

Forgiveness is a powerful practice for setting you free from any difficult emotions that you're holding onto about your body.

For example, you might blame yourself for struggling with your weight for years. Self-blame leaves you feeling unworthy or useless.

Or maybe you're still angry at a family member who constantly put your body down.

Holding onto these feelings can leave you stuck in poor body image, making it difficult to move forward on your journey to better body confidence.

To release yourself from these negative emotions, you firstly need to identify any memories from your past where you felt sad, angry, embarrassed, or humiliated.

Maybe someone told you that you were 'fat' or 'ugly' at school and you felt sad or embarrassed. Or you might have felt angry with yourself when dieting didn't give you the results you wanted.

Make a list of every memory you can think of where you felt bad about your body.

Once you've got your list, for every item on the list, you're going to forgive either **yourself** or any **other person involved**.

The forgiveness practice I'm sharing comes from the Hawaiian practice of reconciliation and forgiveness, or Ho'oponopono.

It may feel strange or uncomfortable at first, but stick with it. To move forward, you need to clear what's blocking you from the past.

For each item say: *"I forgive you. I'm sorry. And I love you."* Don't question the wording, just try it. This doesn't mean that you condone or forget what others might have done to you. It simply means you are releasing negative emotions so you can move on.

Go through every single item, repeating this phrase over and over. Keep going over the list until you no longer experience any emotional charge for each item. Some will go quickly, some will take longer to let go of. But keep going.

Reflection Questions:

What difficult body memories are you choosing to let go of through forgiveness?

How does it feel to forgive yourself? Others?

How does this practice influence your feelings about your body?

Your body is a living miracle, working hard each day to keep you alive – be grateful for that.

50. Be grateful for your body

One of the tools that has helped me most in learning to value and respect my body (and still does), is a regular gratitude practice.

A gratitude practice is a daily habit of acknowledging the things that you feel grateful for.

Being grateful trains your brain to focus on what's positive in your life.

When you practice gratitude, two things happen to your body image.

Firstly, being grateful takes the negative focus off your body. When you're thinking about the good things in your life, you have less room for negative body thoughts.

Secondly, when you are grateful for your body, you begin to experience it more positively, particularly if you focus on its function rather than appearance.

Your body is a good place to be, because it's the only place to be.

So why not start a regular gratitude practice? It's simple to do, but to help you get started, I've got a few ideas for you:

What to be grateful about

They don't have to be big things. In fact, the smaller the better.

You can be grateful for things about your life, like having food on your table.

Or gratitude can be for things about your body, like what your body allows you to do each day e.g. go for a walk, get through a stressful day, or play with your children.

How to practise gratitude

You might begin or end each day writing, thinking, or saying out loud 5-10 things you're grateful for.

You could buy a beautiful notebook, and keep it as your gratitude journal.

Or you might prefer to record a voice note or video each day.

Practise gratitude in whatever way works for you, and notice the difference in your body confidence.

Reflection Questions:

What benefits do you notice by having a gratitude practice?

Feelings will come and go, so help them on their way.

51. Let your feelings out

When you experience negative thoughts and feelings about your body, it's tempting to try to block them out by ignoring them, or turning to your favourite way to comfort yourself whether that's food, alcohol or shopping.

The trouble is, bottling up negative feelings about your body won't help you to feel better.

Instead, allowing your feelings out will help to dissipate their intensity.

When you're experiencing difficult feelings about your body, try saying them out loud, recording them, or writing out what you're really feeling about your body in that moment. Here's something I said to myself recently:

"I really don't like my body today. All these negative feelings about my skin are coming up for me. I'm annoyed with myself that these old feelings are creeping in again, but I know it's perfectly normal to have days like these. The best thing I can do is to acknowledge these feelings and be patient with myself. I know that this feeling will pass."

As well as acknowledging exactly what I was feeling, I also showed myself some compassion by recognising that the way I was feeling is normal, and that I need to be patient with myself.

You might also find it useful to read **Chapter 17- Be self-compassionate** about the importance of self-compassion to better body confidence.

Try releasing your feelings in any way that feels good for you and notice how it makes you feel afterwards.

Reflection Questions:
What way feels most comfortable for you to release your feelings?

How does it feel to let your feelings out?

You get to decide for yourself what success means for YOU.

52. Define what success means for YOU

In a society obsessed with thinness, it's not surprising many women believe that success is about achieving a certain weight or dress size.

When women with good looks and a thin figure are portrayed in the media as 'having it all', it's no wonder that many women tie their self-worth to appearance.

But when you buy into the 'thin ideal', you're caught on a hamster wheel that never stops. The supposed success you seek is always out of reach.

Spending life obsessing over your weight is no way to live. In fact, I'd argue it isn't living at all. Your purpose on this earth is not to achieve a target weight or dress size!

"My actions define my success, not a number on a scale."
Roni Noone

Think of what you could do with all the extra time you'd have if you weren't worrying about your weight or dieting.

You are here to use your own unique brilliance doing things that you enjoy.

When you get to know yourself and what you want from your life, you'll experience a fulfilment that no amount of dieting will ever give you.

It's up to you to define what success means for you. Success doesn't have to mean earning lots of money or becoming famous (although that's okay if that's you!). Success is whatever is important to YOU.

Success might mean spending quality time with your family....

Or taking up a new hobby
Or visiting a country you've always wanted to go to
Or making a change of career
Or being a part of a project or cause close to your heart
Or being a kind and generous person
Or being grateful for the life you have

Take some time to decide what success means for you. Don't take too long to think about it, just write a list of things as they come up, without censoring anything.

Looking at your list, what stands out as being really important to you?

What one thing can you do right away to start moving towards your version of success? For example, if you'd like to support a cause that you care about, what one thing can you do right away to get involved?

Remember that you get to decide what success is for yourself. NOT others.

Reflection Questions:
What does success mean for you?
What, if anything, surprised you about your definition of success?
How are you going to live according to your version of success?

Harnessing the power of your mind, you can *choose* to hate or accept your body.

Afterword

The journey towards body acceptance and appreciation is a challenging, yet hugely rewarding one.

Accepting your body is really an acceptance of self, and all that you are. It's learning to know and like the person inside of you, and recognising your worth outside of your body and appearance.

Your body is your business. You and you alone get to decide how you feel about it.

By harnessing the power of your mind, you can choose to hate your body, or to accept it.

The choice is yours, which will you choose?

"You can spend your life thinking your butt's too big or feeling sexy as hell. Make the choice to appreciate your body as it is."
Victoria Vantoch

From this day forward, I give you full permission to make your own choices about your body.

To help you along your body confidence journey, I invite you to create your own **Body Confidence Manifesto**, to set out how you intend to relate to your body from now on. I've created guidance on how you can do this in the book bonuses, which you can access at:

https://www.heartyourbody.co.uk/little-book-body-confidence-bonuses

Enjoy the journey!

Body confidence is a JOURNEY

not

a destination.

Continue the body confidence journey

If you've enjoyed learning the tools and strategies in this little book, I'd like to invite you to continue your body confidence journey.

I'd be delighted to see you in my Facebook Group, **The Body Confidence Journey**.

This is a community of women who are committed to experiencing greater comfort and joy in their bodies.

Using the link below, you can request to join this closed and confidential community:

www.facebook.com/groups/thebodyconfidencejourney

Don't forget to grab the bonuses that come with this book over at:

https://www.heartyourbody.co.uk/little-book-body-confidence-bonuses

Recommended reading

When I started out on my body confidence journey, I read every book on body image and confidence I could lay my hands on.

I got to the crux of what body image was and discovered practical ways that I could see my body in a more positive light.

As you do your own research and become more informed about body image, it will help your body confidence grow.

If you're looking for some good books to get you started, I'd recommend the following:

The Body Image Workbook by Thomas F Cash.

Love your Body, Love your Life by Sarah Maria.

Mirror, Mirror by Dr Linda Papadopoulos.

The Goddess Revolution by Mel Wells.

Body Image Remix by Summer Innanen.

There is Nothing Wrong with You: A Compassionate

Process for Learning to Accept Yourself Exactly as You Are by Cheri Huber.

The Tapping Solution for Weight Loss & Body Confidence: A Woman's Guide to Stressing Less, Weighing less and Loving More by Jessica Ortner.

I Heart Me: The Science of Self-Love by David R Hamilton PhD.

Health at Every Size – The Surprising Truth about Your Weight by Linda Bacon PhD.

Bibliography

Fat Talk and Body Image Disturbance – A Systematic Review and Meta-Analysis. **Psychology of Women Quarterly.** Jacqueline Mills, Matthew Fuller-Tyszkiewicz.

Kristin Neff PhD. **Self-Compassion: Stop Beating Yourself Up and Leave Insecurity Behind.**

Action for Happiness. **The 10 Keys to Happier Living** by Vanessa King.

Centre for Appearance Research. **Appearance Matters Podcast – Episode 15 – Body Image & Mindfulness.**

Anthony Robbins. **Unlimited Power – The New Science of Personal Achievement.**

Dr Aric Sigman. **The Body Wars – Why body dissatisfaction is at epidemic proportions and how we can fight back.**

About the author

Judi is a coach specialising in women's body image, helping her clients to accept and respect their bodies so they can live happier, healthier and more fulfilling lives.

It's Judi's mission to help as many women as possible kick the body hate habit and start living the life they truly desire.

Judi lives on the South Coast of the UK with her husband Chris and her extensive Jelly Cat collection.

Connect with Judi

Find out more about Judi and her work at:

www.heartyourbody.co.uk

Judi can also be found on the following social media:

www.facebook.com/heartyourbodyuk

www.twitter.com/heartyourbodyuk

Printed in Poland
by Amazon Fulfillment
Poland Sp. z o.o., Wrocław